This book is about: THE PERSECUTION OF NJWEEDMAN

"Jury Nullification – Medical Marijuana – Legalization"

Ed Forchion knows what it's like to be caught between a rock and a hard place. There are two major dramas that have played out in the prime of his life: His battle against the system that tried—and for a time succeeded—in putting him away "in a cage because of a plant," and, simultaneously, his battle against his own body, which was in revolt and threatening to consume him.

This is a medical marijuana horror story in three acts: A medical marijuana patient comes from California to New Jersey for a visit and is arrested with marijuana. During the course of his trials and tribulations, the prosecutor calls him a Charlatan, and the judge accuses him of playing his health like a Stradivarius. And NJ is supposed to be a medical marijuana state—even though the governor is resisting it and the qualifications are most restrictive—and it does not recognize the rights of out-of-state patients.

There are three fronts in this war on marijuana Social use, medical use and spirit use. I belong to all three fronts. I am a legalizer, who happens to have bone cancer and believes in the spiritual use of the herb!

I've been persecuted for years for knowing the truth, telling the truth to others and refusing to complying with the lies. These LIE LAWS were passed by our all white Congress's in 1937 with the Marijuana Taxation Act and re-inforced in 1970 with the Controlled Substance Act. These laws are nothing but Racist inspired legislation used to enslave us. While I know poor whites are arrested for marijuana too it is a fact they are the collateral damage of this racist war. They weren't the intended victims of these original racist laws.

The war on marijuana has been won by "We the People" but our politicians like Gov Christopher Christie refuse to surrender. So we must take our victory, we must take to the streets and stop allowing these tyrants to imprison us in their new age concrete plantation systems.

Jah Bless - NJWeedman"

This is an interactive web-book and a regular book. Click on all pictures and links or type them in directly. This book is designed to be read while (HIGH) infront of computer, or in kindle version.

Robert Edward Forchion, Jr – aka- is a African American former Political Prisoner of the State of New Jersey. He is a medical marijuana activist, author, columnist, Thc-Intellectual.

http://en.wikipedia.org/wiki/NJWEEDMAN

The Politics of Pot

New Jersey

Style

X-Ray Showing Forchion's Cancerous Bone Tumors

Judge Delehey

Edward Forchion is a legitimate Medical Marijuana Bone Cancer patient.
Judge Delehey says, "He has played his health as if it was a Stradivarius."

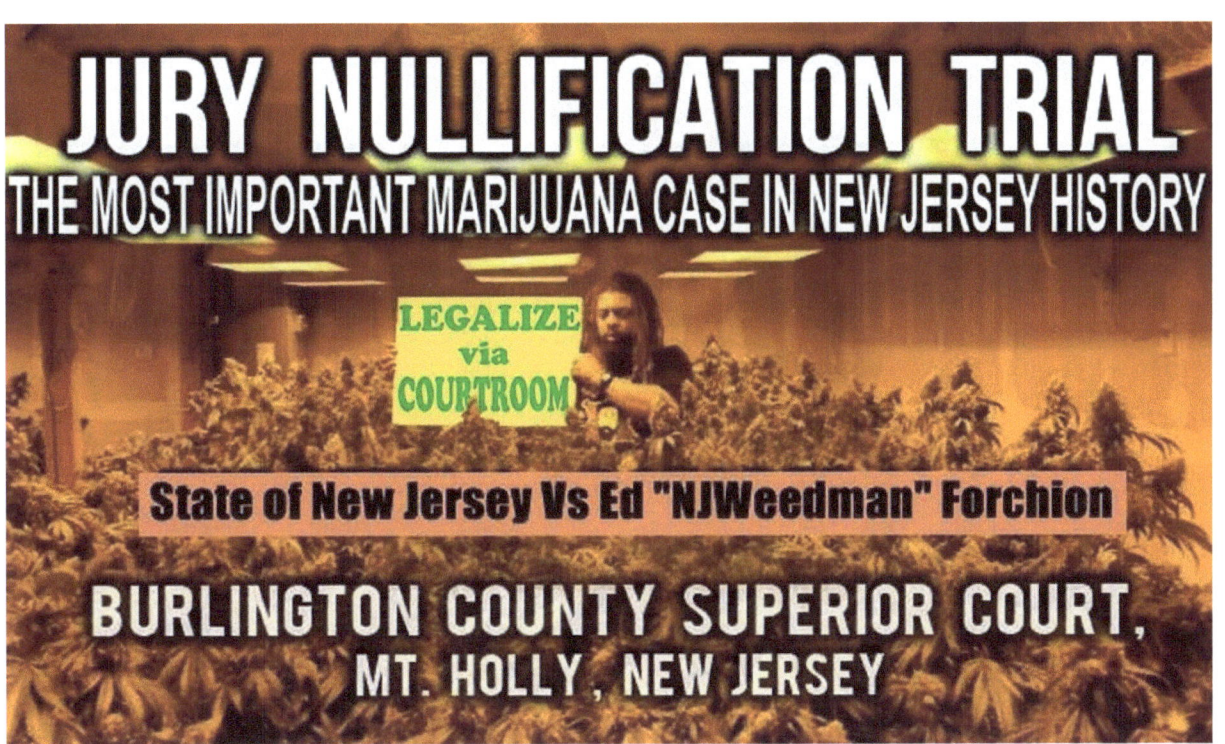

New Jersey Appeals Court case # A-004052-12T4

DECISION AWAITS at time of Publication

Act 1

Early 1990s: Based in New Jersey, coast-to-coast truck driver Ed Forchion is dubbed Weedman (already known as Jersey) when he snubbed the prospect of transporting other drugs beyond marijuana amid his regular shipments. He proudly admits that he was smuggling marijuana from Arizona to New Jersey. Though the Mexican drug dealers he picked up from called him "JERSEY," his refusal to transport anything but marijuana would ultimately get them calling him "JERSEYWEEDMAN."

By 1994 he was still in the cannabis closet: He had acquired his first relevant screen name online, "NJweedman," but his truck number was 519—one digit up and one digit down from 420.

The shit first hit the fan on November 24, 1997, when he was arrested in Belmawr, New Jersey, by the Camden County Drug Task Force, as well as state, county, and DEA task force agents, for possessing 40 pounds of marijuana. (www.njweedman.com/arrest.htm)

Edward Forchion, of Browns Mills, takes a reefer break at the State House Thursday.

His response to the arrest? On April 20, 1998, Forchion formed the Legalize Marijuana Party with him at the helm and announces he is running for Congress, which is the beginning of his campaign to spread awareness about jury nullification (the right of jurors to acquit a defendant if they do not agree with the law in question). "I knew about it since I was a little kid because I used to read," says Forchion. "My mom made me do a book report on William Penn when I was 12 years old." (http://www.njweedman.com/ed_nullify.htm)

It took three years to get to trial. During those three years he went on a campaign of smoking weed in public places, he made numerous statements, and he publicly advocated jury nullification. He even smoked a joint in the State House in front of the entire State Assembly. (see image)

JOINT LEGISLATIVE SESSION

Activist Lights Up in Assembly /P.5

"Most people read everything from left to right. I also read things from right to left."

"The Miranda Rights state that anything you say can and will be used against you. I know there is a reciprocal to everything, so it could also be made to work for you. The prosecution wants to say marijuana is dangerous, so I figured I would run for office and talk about legalization, and pollute the jury pool with the knowledge of truth. I wanted my jurors to know who I was. I wanted to have an OJ trial—I wanted members of the jury to feel for me."

Maybe I was before my time a little because I was sure it was time to people used Jury Nullification to end the prohibition on marijuana. I wasn't crazy.

Jury nullification *occurs in a trial when a jury acquits a defendant, even though the members of the jury believe the defendant to be guilty of the charges. This may occur when members of the jury disagree with the law the defendant has been charged with breaking, or believe that the law should not be applied in that particular case. A jury can similarly convict a defendant on the ground of disagreement with an existing law.* I thought who the fuck believes the lies about marijuana. I thought I could get 1 on my jury who wasn't stupid!

Back then people told Forchion he was talking his way into jail. Nonetheless, in 1998 he ran for Congress and in 1999 for State Assembly; in 2000 he ran for Congress again, and additionally ran for Camden County Freeholder in 1998 and 1999 and ran for Burlington County Freeholder in 2000. Though he ran for two offices in a given year at the outset, since then the rules have changed and it is not possible to run for multiple offices. He first ran as Edward Robert Forchion, then Edward NJWeedman Forchion. In 2000 the Camden County Court Clerk refused to put NJWeedman on the ballot; the Attorney General's office chimed in, and he was not allowed to use that name. I did all that for one reason only, to make myself know to the public and my potential jurors.

Forchion's trial—the first of three—got under way on September 18, 2000. In the interim he had been in TV commercials and talked about his case in newspapers, all the while slowly going broke: 10 days after the 1997 arrest, sheriffs showed up to repossess Forchion's truck, which was significant because the sheriff's department had told the company that held the lien on Forchion's truck that he had been arrested, but he had bailed out about four days later and remained free awaiting trial. "Your chances of winning a case are better when you're on the outside than on the inside. From outside you're able to pollute the jury," he says. "When I went to trial three years later, some members of the jury made the mistake of telling the judge ahead of time that they would not be able to find me guilty rather than simply performing the nullification." However, since the lien holder had been told Forchion was in jail, the sheriffs were able to seize the truck. "Not only did I get arrested, and it cost me a whole bunch of money to get out, they came and took my truck, my means of making legal money. It didn't take long: In less than a year, I lost my house. So I was angry. In 1998 I was the angriest black man in South Jersey."

For three years while he awaited trial he ran for office, called in to talk shows, drove around the first incarnation of the Weedmobil (which at that time had statements and stickers in place of the art that would come to embellish the present-day Weedmobil). "I polluted the jury pool in Camden County. Everyone knew who I was and many agreed the marijuana laws were wrong and if they were on my jury they would find me "*not guilty.*" I just needed one juror to agree with me. In the middle of the trial, I had members of the jury nodding their head at me while I spoke." He adds that the prosecutor was actually "a pretty cool guy" who would later tell Forchion that although he was obligated to perform the duties of his job, he did actually like him. "I was the most interesting person he attempted to prosecute, because I knew how to operate in the system."

The Heart of Jury Nullification

And yet, Forchion's desperate arguments—and his undeniable charisma—appeared to have some effect. One juror started crying after his compelling opening statement, insisting she couldn't convict him. She got tossed from the jury because the judge said she had no objectivity and was not open to deliberation. "The replacement juror was a nun—with a habit and everything," recalls Forchion. She started crying too, but she said she was open to hearing the case objectively and wasn't thrown off. That's when, on the third day of trial, Camden County prosecutor John Wynne offered Forchion a deal—a 10-year flat sentence, which came with the stipulation that he'd be out and placed into ISP (Intensive Supervision Program) within three to six months. "I felt sorry for him and I felt that he was definitely going to get convicted," says Wynne, who's now a criminal defense attorney. "I gave him a sweetheart deal because he's a nice guy, a hard worker, he's got kids, he's got support obligations, and I felt he shouldn't go to prison for a long time."

But Wynne also admits the notion that Forchion's jury nullification strategy could actually work—perhaps setting a precedent for other similar cases—also played into his decision to extend the deal. "I didn't want the jury to say that the drug law was not good," says Wynne. "There was always a chance that they would, and my attitude was, why risk that?" (Read more about this part of Forchion's story at: http://tinyurl.com/dearaid)

Forchion asserts: "I said I would only take a deal if I could poll the jury about how they would have voted. It was unusual, but the judge was curious too, which he even said, and he allowed it. Five were in favor. From 1997 to 2000 I was adamant I would not take a deal. The newspapers said I was on a crazy suicide mission. They followed me for three years because I was the dude with the big balls who was gonna fight this thing. I had refused several pre-trial plea deals. And here I was being offered a deal. I took the deal and then learned I had five jurors on my side." I always regretted that deal, I felt I hadn't been true to myself, my own beliefs and open proclamations. I was embarrassed I'd taken that deal after all the jury nullification speeches.

And so he went to prison. The deal was that the state would drop its first-degree charge for which he was facing 20 years if convicted to a deal where he was to serve 3 to 6 months and then be released as part of ISP. However, the deal would soon be reneged on. "You can't trust the system is what I'm saying."

December 1, 2000: Forchion begins serving time at Riverfront State Prison in Camden, New Jersey. Around January 6, 2001, Forchion received a letter from ISP: He was being informed that he was ineligible to participate in the release program and would have to serve out the flat 10-year sentence called for in the deal. "For three years they thought I was crazy—until I started having jurors crying in my favor. Until I got to trial I didn't know what was going to happen. I was in the dark. The prosecution thought I was crazy at first—by the second and third trial they knew I had jurors on my side, but at this first one I was taking a chance and gambling on a sentence." Any amount over 25 pounds is a first-degree crime, which comes with a 20-year sentence. "The State blinked, they offered me a flat sentence and what they call ISP. I blinked too—I accepted. As far as I was concerned, they bribed me with leniency for guilty testimony against myself. But I took the deal." Though he later tried to withdraw his plea, he was unable to do so, and he had to report to prison on December 1 of 2000.

Just days later, his right knee begins to hurt something fierce. Some amount of pain had been present for about a year; he thought it stemmed from an injury sustained while in the army, or perhaps an old sports injury. After all, he was in his thirties at that point and figured life was just catching up with him, that he should chill out a bit. So he had stopped playing ball and gone about his business. Now here he was in prison and there was pain that couldn't be ignored, but no visible signs of anything amiss.

"I was flipping out, stuck in jail with a flat sentence. Even though I was eligible for other programs, I thought I'd be out in 3 to 6 months. Long story short, they reneged on the deal. They bamboozled me. They got me to plead guilty, and they reneged on the deal. No one can hear you scream while you're in jail." He wrote letters and tried to withdraw his plea since the court had reneged. No one would hear him.

"I could have set a precedent if I'd been successful. [Prosecutor] John Lynn was scared. These are Ivy League Cornell types, and I'm outmaneuvering them in court. That is why he offered the deal."

Diagnosed with Bone Cancer While in Prison

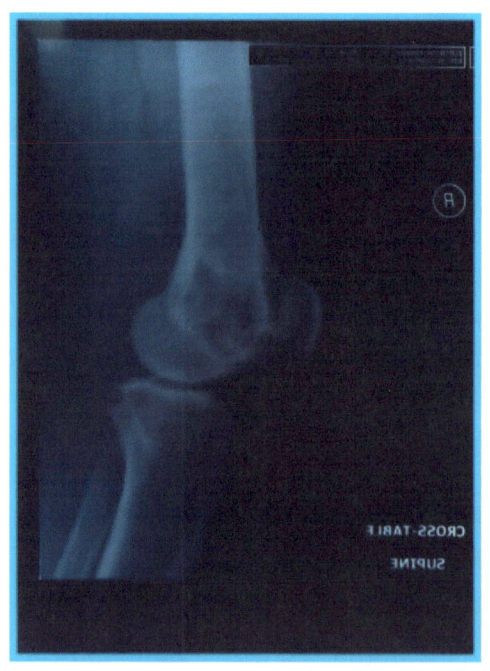

By February 2001 the intensifying pain in Forchion's knee was accompanied by a visible lump. It was hot and a network of new blood vessels had cropped up around it. He would see the prison nurse, explain his situation, and be given an aspirin and told to go back to his cell. "I knew something was wrong here, I could see veins." For over a month nothing was done for him. From prison Forchion reached out to Dr. Steven Fenichel, who happens to be an outspoken proponent of medical marijuana, and told him something serious was going on. "The doctor came in as a regular visitor, sat down, pulled up my pants and looked at my knee. He compared legs and right away told me, 'Don't panic, but I think you've got a sarcoma growing on your bone.'" Dr. Fenichel left and immediately called the warden and informed him there is a guy with a serious health issue in the prison. Afterward he contacted a number of state officials in Trenton who were also alerted of his condition. Finally Forchion was transported to a hospital to see an oncologist. "He said, 'Oh yeah, you've got a tumor growing on your leg.' I was like, no shit, it's half the size of a golf ball by now."

In April 2001 X-rays confirmed the mass as a tumor, but blood tests showed no significant deviation from normal bodily levels—it wasn't showing up as cancer. For eight months Forchion endured the horror of feeling something growing within him, something that could destroy him more thoroughly than the system could ever hope to. "It's horrible to be imprisoned by inadequate health care as well."

A biopsy was scheduled in May but the appointment was missed. "I was waiting and waiting one morning, but they never came to transport me. I bitched, the doctors bitched. I was supposed to go June 10 for the follow-up, which I missed also. No explanation, they just didn't transport me. Doctors didn't see me in July because the biopsy was not done, so there was no reason for the appointment if we couldn't come up with a plan." Finally in August a surgery and a biopsy were scheduled for the same day. At this point Forchion still doesn't know if the tumor is malignant or benign. The biopsy would later reveal: This was a giant cell tumor, a rare condition—though painful, this kind of tumor is not generally fast growing and has a low mortality rate (around 10%, unless the tumor is cut out and subsequently recurs elsewhere in the body—in which case the rate goes up). The fact that it had cropped up on his leg was a boon—if it develops on the lung or skull it can be fatal. It has the potential to metastasize and travel through the body via the blood. And surgery would not necessarily be the end of the matter: One of the dangers of getting the tumor cut out is that the cancer can still come back, and if it doesn't come back in the same spot, it could resurface in a dangerous region.

The Lord Helps Those Who Help Themselves: NJWeedman.com

While in prison, Forchion had corresponded with a friend in Florida who'd previously talked him through learning HTML. "I started my website in 1998 with the help of James Dawson, a medical marijuana patient and activist I met at a Philadelphia conference. So from prison I had it put on my home page that I was bamboozled with regard to the deal that was reneged on, and I filed a motion to change my name to njweedman.com." He mailed the name change petition to several news outlets. *The Trentonian* was the first to write about it. *The Star ledger,* the AP, *Maxim*—a host of others followed suit. "No one was listening to me about how the court reneged and bamboozled me on the deal, but I explained the whole thing on my site. That was the real reason I wanted to change my name to that." He filed that motion to change his name as a way of reaching the outside press. A month after petitioning the court to change his name, a move that garnered attention across the nation, Forchion gets a letter from ISP saying they've changed their mind. (The website cast ISP, "the state," in a bad light.) He also motioned to withdraw the plea deal since the state had reneged on the deal by not giving him ISP. He'd spent 17 months in jail, from December 1, 2001, to April 3, 2002. "They (the state) gave me the ISP program rather than have to admit they were wrong and go back to trial."

CENSORSHIP—POLITICAL IMPRISONMENT

I was imprisoned for 5 months for speaking out about the politics of pot
(http://tinyurl.com/NJWcensorship)

New Jersey marijuana activist Ed "NJ Weedman" Forchion

"I was the angriest man in America in 1998/99 before I was imprisoned, but I became the angriest man in the world in 2002 when I got out of jail, after they had reneged on me and everything." He'd spent three years talking to the press, the name change matter was still going on through the New Jersey Appeals court. He was highly motivated to speak out against the marijuana laws. His parole officer, Thomas Bartlett, orders him not to talk about pot, to which he responds, "I can talk about anything I want. I don't check my constitutional rights at the prison gate, and I am not even in prison anymore. I can talk about whatever I want in there, it's an example of my First Amendment rights." He adds, "I complained to the U.S. Attorney's office in Newark that this state official Thomas Bartlett was threatening to put me in jail if I didn't stop talking about marijuana! I got a letter from the fat twit's office that they found my allegations unfounded."

"Thomas Bartlett, a born-again Christian WHO DIDN'T LIKE MY OPINIONS ON MARIJUANA, then had me thrown in the Burlington County jail for 4 days in June 2002, until I promised not to talk about marijuana anymore. I was so so pissed at this and I developed a plan."

"I made three commercials from my point of view that were like a big fuck you to Bartlett. I was playing my trump card—you think I can't talk to the press?" This provoked anger in Bartlett and the NJ courts; a warrant was obtained for Forchion's arrest in August. Forchion says Judge Giovine rubber-stamped whatever Bartlett the officer said: he alleged that Forchion was advocating criminal activity by talking about legalization and changing law—despite disagreement with a law being free speech, one of the fundamental pillars of our democracy. "At this point I wasn't even saying 'Fuck the law, smoke it anyway.' I deliberately started saying that afterward, that's the reason I start off every speech with that statement."

ED FORCHION
1ST AMENDMENT ACTIVIST

Now in the Burlington County jail and facing the prospect of serving out a 10-year sentence, Forchion filed a "writ of habeas corpus" and mailed it to a clerk of a federal judge in Camden County. He relates that he is in jail for making commercials, which is a violation of his right to free speech and his right to disagree with the government. (First Amendment Right to Redress of Grievances) Federal Judge Joseph Irenas calls for evidentiary hearings to be held, after which it comes to light that Forchion is right. Five months later the judge rules in his favor.

(http://tinyurl.com/NJWispCensorship) Although a federal judge is not supposed to intercede until all state claims and appeals have been exhausted, this judge said the matter constituted an egregious act, that it would take Forchion six years to exhaust all his claims. The state Attorney General's office fought the matter, saying it did not fall within the jurisdiction of a federal judge. Nonetheless, 45 days later Federal Judge Irena's affirmed that he did have the power to exercise federal jurisdiction because the Feldman-Rooker doctrine that prohibits federal courts below the Supreme Court from sitting in direct review of a state court decision without the authorization of Congress did not apply to this case, so it was ordered that Forchion be released.

"When I tried to file criminal civil rights violations charges against the ISP officer Thomas Bartlett for having me put in jail in the first place, I was told by the Federal Judge that only the U.S. Attorney's Office was empowered to do that. So I went to meet this twit..."

This Is How I Came to Know Christopher Christie, then the U.S. Attorney

(picture credit – nj.com?)

Forchion tries to charge the ISP officials with a crime. "There's already a statute about it. I screamed bloody murder but no one took me seriously. I spent five months in jail [that time]." He approached the man who would later become our present governor—Chris Christie, back when he was the U.S. Attorney for NJ. In July 2003 a letter came from Christie's office informing Forchion that the claim had been investigated and criminal charges would not be pursued against the officials. "I called him a fat hypocrite. Every Monday I had off from work, so I went and stood in front of his office with a sign that said 'fat hypocrite,' because he was not going after law-breaking state officials, which he vowed was his mission. (http://www.njweedman.com/hypocrite.html) He didn't go for it because it was me, and I was saying legalize it. Because it was about marijuana, he was not going to come to my aid." The judge granted the officers immunity, but that was for a civil suit, not a criminal matter. That was up to Christie, and he declined to pursue it. "So I made a sign. I passed out letters explaining why I thought Christie was a fat hypocrite. And I got arrested. At first the regular guards at the door came out and said I had to leave. I said 'I'm on public property, and hell no I'm not leaving.' After another warning 15 minutes later, the what I call Goon Squad guys from upstairs came to get me—all black uniforms, boots, Kevlar, guns on their hips. I still wouldn't leave, so they grabbed me, arrested me, and took me in. They said I was trespassing—you can't trespass on federal property. It's ours. Trespassing, disorderly conduct—Ms. Paula Dow, the Essex County Prosecutor, became my witness. They arrested me twice that first day, and held me until 6 P.M." Next Monday, Forchion had off from work again. "I was there for about 20 minutes before they arrested me. This time they banged me all around. They didn't punch me, but they banged me into everything they could, and I didn't get hurt but it did hurt." They held him from 11 in the morning until 6 in the evening. Of course Forchion came back the following Monday. "Four weeks in a row I showed up to call Christie a fat hypocrite."

"UNDER A WATCHFUL EYE"

By Jim Edwards, **August 11, 2003** - Ed Forchion, better known as "the Weedman," loves publicity almost as much as he loves marijuana. Last Monday, (AUGUST 4th,) he was arrested during a protest outside the U.S. Attorney's Office in Newark, and he called a variety of newspapers in case they missed it.

Normally, this would not be worthy of note; Forchion has a history of arrests during similar pro-marijuana legalization protests. But on Monday, the incident had an unusually prominent witness - counsel to the U.S. Attorney, Paula Dow. "She was very nice," says Forchion, who didn't know who she was at the time.

The theme of the protest was that U.S. Attorney Christopher Christie is a "hypocrite" because he hasn't investigated the state officials who jailed Forchion after he made legalization protests during his post-conviction supervision last year. Forchion won a habeas suit in federal district court that ruled that jailing illegal.

"I met him for a short period," Dow confirms. "I wanted to find out if anything was happening improperly . . . I didn't see anything."

Forchion, who says he will plead not guilty to charges of creating a disturbance, soliciting and vending, and nonconformity with signs and directions, argues that he has a First Amendment right to hold a sign and distribute fliers outside the federal building. His court date is Oct. 30; he faces fines totaling $150. **-- New Jersey Law Journal**

Forchion could not find any lawyer who wanted to take up the mantle of this lawsuit. Not the U.S. Attorney of NJ, no one, wanted to be the guy to take on the most powerful federal official in New Jersey. He never did get to file that Bivens lawsuit against "Fat-Fuck Christie." But the federal judge yelled at the U.S. Attorney who got sent to represent Christie. The judge gave the attorney the opportunity to dismiss the case, and when he didn't the judge dismissed it himself and proceeded to yell at the attorney, asking him if he understood the First Amendment and stating that this incident happened right outside the building—the Martin Luther King Building and U.S. Courthouse, and this was clearly a First Amendment issue. The judge was familiar with Forchion's cases, and he slammed the prosecution. The prosecution said they'd only dismiss the charge if Forchion agreed not to file a Bivens action against the federal officials. So then judge just dismissed it himself, and no Bivens waiver was issued. No one would help him sue anyone. Though Forchion never sent anything threatening to Christie in the mail (although there was that article he wiped his ass with…), off and on for a number of years—even from out in LA—Forchion would send him some marijuana along with his correspondence. (And cc reporters with the same letter and attachment!)

"Chicken Little Christie, the sky's not falling," says Forchion. "Things were great in California with legal weed, but in NJ he acts like the sky would fall if we legalize it."

NO YOU CAN'T HAVE MY DNA—KISS MY ASS & SWAB YOUR LIPS

But another battle was brewing: In 2003 a law was passed requiring all state prisoners to submit a sample of their DNA. Forchion receives a letter in the mail saying he must comply. "Remember, I was the angriest black man in world then. 'I refuse, kiss my ass, and retrieve the DNA from your lips,' I wrote, and mailed a picture of my ass to the New Jersey Attorney General and Governor McGreevey. So the State filed criminal contempt charges. I had gotten a letter the first week after the law took effect because I had already made myself a famous criminal." He was in the newspapers every couple weeks; he keeps scrapbooks of all articles about him. And he had just beaten the state on the censorship case. He took out the provocative statement from the letter he sent to the attorney general and the governor and sent that to the same federal court judge—Judge Irenas—as another "WRIT of HABEAS CORPUS," stating this was an attempt to punish him unfairly, the most prominent reason being that it was an ex post facto law. He challenged the DNA law as unconstitutional. "The law was passed in September of 2003, so that was not the law when I plead guilty in September of 2000, and I refused to comply with it. If they were going to force me to do this, I found it so egregious that I wanted to go back to trial. I motioned again to withdraw my original plea. I wanted to go back to trial and complete the prosecution that was interrupted by the acceptance of the plea deal. My reasoning was the deal had been broken by the state, so I wanted to withdraw my plea. Instead, the state withdrew. They didn't want to go back to trial because they didn't want to lose—they saw the jury was on my side. And I had over 40 pounds at that time!" The DNA case was written up in law journals across the country. "To me it was a two-pronged case: a 'kiss my ass' to the state, and legal arguments to the feds about whether it is unconstitutional. Federal Judge Irenas issued an injunction against statewide DNA collection. The state indicted Forchion for criminal contempt within a week of his refusal to surrender his DNA—unprecedentedly fast. "The NJWeedman rules: I get treated different all the time in NJ courts, it has been like that for 15 years."

Ultimately the appellate court ruled that Forchion didn't have to give up his DNA, so the federal judge lifted the injunction. The state was then allowed to proceed with its new DNA law, and Forchion didn't have to give up his DNA. "I tried to tell lawyers, but no one cared. There was a whole class of prisoners and citizens being forced to give up their DNA, and I was exempted just to remove my standing in the federal injunction. Once the state appeals court said I didn't have to give up my DNA, I had no standing to argue in federal court that the DNA law was unconstitutional.

NJWeedman Rolls Up Victories in Court

Monica Yate Kinney
Inquirer Columnist

The Weedman smokes on.

When we last checked in with the dreadlocked crusader for free speech and the right to light up, he was fighting a fistful of federal lawsuits and mounting a U.S. House campaign. The Weedman – real name: Edward Forchion – was also desperately trying to keep himself out of jail.

Apparently the Camden County Prosecutor's Office hadn't looked too kindly on the Weedman's refusal to deposit his DNA into the state's criminal gene bank. I must admit, I worried about the Weedman during my months at home with baby Jane.

He's my favorite former felon. He gives great copy.

And he may be the only political candidate in New Jersey history with the guts to put a picture of himself mooning the governor on his website. Miraculously, after a lifetime of toking, the Weedman has retained enough brain cells to render him one heck of an unlicensed legal eagle.

Last year he got his parole-violation sentence overturned after convincing a federal judge that officials had locked him up to squelch his constitutional right to proselytize about pot. This fall the Weedman beat the rap on that DNA case.

And last month, a federal judge considering the Rastafarian's quest to conduct smoky sacraments outside Independence Hall paid the pothead a compliment in open court. Had Mr. Forchion ever considered going to law school, the judge asked. He might have missed his calling.

The name game:

We reunite at a Burlington County McDonald's. The Weedman orders a chicken salad and fries. He has a case of the marijuana munchies but plenty of time to bring me up to speed on his exploits.

Bad news: He lost the fight to change his name to NJWeedman.com. The court said the new name would promote a criminal enterprise. Silly judges. Publicity and provocation, not sales, are his profession.

Now the proud black man is considering filing papers to legally become Just A. Nigga. Just to tick people off.

As we chat, a stranger stops by our booth to make a celebrity sighting. "Are you..." he asks in awe, "...the actual Weedman?"

The Weedman nods, and stuffs campaign flyers into his fan's hand.

The dude pledges to vote for the Weedman, who is running on the Marijuana Party ticket against U.S. Rep Jim Saxton. Forchion knows he's going to need a lot more McDonald's moments to unseat the incumbent.

After clashing with Comcast over his campaign ads, the Weedman finally managed to put a few of them on TV over the summer. But he had only $1,000 to spend.

He'll have to raise more money next time around. "I'm a gadfly," he explains, perhaps to the cable company's horror. "I'm going to run for office every year."

Fame and Forchion:

Alas, neither fame nor infamy has translated into fortune for Forchion.

Over the summer, the oft-unemployed father of four finally landed a job as a courier. Ironically, the job required him to deliver documents to the state justice officials he has mocked mercilessly. He made $600 a week – completely legit! – but not for long. In August, a couple of weeks after Gov. McGreevey's "I am a gay American" speech, the Weedman delivered an address of his own, right on the State House steps in Trenton. As usual, the cameras were rolling.

His bosses caught the show. And, like clockwork, the Weedman lost a job and found another fight. He promptly filed a wrongful-termination suit, alleging he was fired for expressing political views.

McMeal finished, the Weedman says he has to get back to politicking. He is, blessedly, a one-issue candidate. He just wants to end the drug war and legalize marijuana.

"How is it that the only way an average guy can get his voice heard today," he asks before climbing into his beat-up van, "is by taking advantage of election laws?"

In 2004 the DNA matter is behind him. In 2005 he gets his truck back. "I was kicked off ISP, I'd already beaten the state on a couple of things, I stayed in prison longer than when they reneged on the ISP deal, but I came up with an ingenious way to put the spotlight on the state with the name change, and I got out. The program officer Bartlett was a dickhead, I got into a pissing contest with ISP that ended up in federal court. No one expected that, and  certainly no one expected I would win. And the DNA—fuck you, I ain't gonna give you my DNA. I won that one, too. It took a little longer, but I also follow with statute 1983 federal lawsuit against the ISP officers—no ISP officer wanted to deal with me. 'He's suing everyone and winning.' I should never have taken that deal. I took it because they agreed to let me poll the jury. When I found out I had five jurors on my side, I was angry at myself." He was let off ISP on December 6, 2003, without having to remain on parole for the required 20 months. "They wanted nothing more to do with me. They let me go. I was kicked outta parole, and I didn't have to give my DNA to the state."

That same month Forchion starts his most high-profile protest and gets national attention. The smoke-outs in Philadelphia: He smoked joints at the Liberty Bell, which turns into a federal case. (http://www.njweedman.com/smokeout.html)

His father had helped him get his truck back, so in 2005 Forchion is a truck driver again. "I let it go. I was angry, but at least I was free to travel the country again. I still got my name on the ballot a couple times, Senate in 2005 and Gov in 2006, but they were just spiteful acts. My way of continuing to give the finger to the Democrats and Republicans who created these stupid marijuana laws." Articles on him highlighted how remarkable it was that he wins everything pro se. He'd begun driving a truck again. He walked away from the name change matter. He won the federal "smoke-out" case in Philadelphia—the case was thrown out. That may have been the end of the NJWeedman, story but it wasn't.

Act 2

In 2007 he and his second wife get a divorce. Forchion moves to California seeking Political Asylum. "Fuck Jersey I said—I'm still NJWeedman, I still have the website, the media still covers me. Now I'm in LA safe from the politics of Pot Jersey Style, with a history of fighting the system working for me, and the Rastas lovin' me. I did well out there."

"Within a few months I opened my own marijuana dispensary on Hollywood Blvd. called the Liberty Bell Temple. I started my own party promotions "Njweedman Promotions" and held huge marijuana-themed parties, including one honoring the election of the leader of the Choom Gang as President of the United States of America. I became a Hollywood personality, even appearing on TMZ three times in 2010. https://www.youtube.com/watch?v=DIOyQHXp2II

He comes back to New Jersey every other month to visit his family. On one such visit he gets arrested—April 1, 2010. "I got out of jail on April 4. I felt like this was Déjà Vu, and I made a vow in front of the NJ State Police headquarters that I was going to fight this case and do it all over again. This time I was going all the way to trial. Remembering the deal for ISP made during the first trial in 2000, which was then reneged on, I was adamant. There would be no deals—this was going to trial."

"I was going to encourage my Jury to Nullify the law and find me NOT GUILTY. (https://vimeo.com/24099651) I was back in the safety of California by April 10, 2010, and I vowed to challenge the law constitutionally."

He had a history of presenting constitutional arguments to the courts and winning. This time the judge and the prosecutors complained and called on the DEA in Los Angeles to help out the State of New Jersey against him.

"I was winning the PR war, the people don't believe the LIES about marijuana the government portrays, the state prosecutors knew I had the public's attention, and they knew I knew about Jury Nullification. Eventually the DEA destroyed me at the behest of State of New Jersey officials. It's like winning a fight on the playground, and the loser tells his big brother to go after the winner. Uncle Sam comes and beats me up. Takes all my money in an attempt by the government to defund me, to make it impossible to fight. It was an attempt to keep me from being able to hire witnesses and experts to support my defense at trial."

He had left NJ and went to Cali for political and personal reasons. "I was gonna have a hard time being in New Jersey and not being angry. I didn't want to be divorced, I knew my marijuana activism contributed greatly to my wife's desire to get divorced. Among the things I did wrong also was the glaring fact that she didn't want to be Mrs. NJWeedman—it had become too much for her. When I left I said I'd come home every other month for 7 to 10 days. I was in the papers in 2006 for: quitting weed, driving the truck, divorcing. Making headlines: Weedman's going to Hollywood."

"Life was grand in Hollywood, I called it my E! True Hollyweed Story: From Camden County Jail to Hollywood Boulevard—I was on TV, in movies, livin' it up, making the scene. I published a book *PUBLIC ENEMY #420* on January 18, 2010—ironically on the same day New Jersey legalized medical marijuana."

"Then I came home for that visit and *bam*."

Busted on April 1, 2010, with a pound of marijuana, Forchion finds himself in and out of court. He had been pulling in $100,000 a year with access to double and triple that from his professional endeavors (which largely included being the proprietor of The Liberty Bell Temple II, spending upwards of $10,000 on commercials, paying child support, maintaining multiple cars).

"TV producers were talking to me prior to the December 2011 DEA raid. I even had a shot at being on *Pot Wars*—my shop was supposed to be bringing some color to it, Rasta flavor, characters. Then the DEA came and smashed me. Discovery and Nat Geo still wanted to give me a reality show for a minute. Trials, jail. No deals, punching all the way. I starred in the documentary *HOW WEED WON THE WEST,* appeared on the Supreme Court of Comedy, and played myself on a couple episodes of *1,000 Ways to Die.*"

"Prosecutions in Jersey are slow. My California life proceeded from the safety of California…or so I thought I fought."

"I filed a Constitutional Challenge to the New Jersey medical marijuana laws on 4/20/2011 (read about it here: http://tinyurl.com/NJWchallenge).

Burlington County Assistant Prosecutor Michael Luciano's state reply brief 6/30/2011 (read about it here: http://tinyurl.com/prosecutorReply)

JUDGE DELEHEY DENIES CHALLENGE MOTION – http://tinyurl.com/DeleheyDenies

This denial sets up this case to be appealed no matter what the verdict and thus likely sets up this case as test case on the new landscape of marijuana law in New Jersey. This case became the most important marijuana case in the history of New Jersey with this denial. "*I regard this as the greatest set up ever in the marijuana movement for a case to be the Roe Vs Wade case of marijuana*".

(SEND2PRESS NEWSWIRE)

Mt Holly, NJ. – 4/18/2011 As medical marijuana smokers around the globe celebrate "4/20" – an internationally recognized date for the celebration of cannabis – Ed Forchion, aka NJWeedman,  announced that his lawyer, John Vincent Saykanic, Esq., will be filing a historic legal brief in New Jersey's Burlington County Superior Court, battling for not only Forchion's freedom but for the rights and recognition of marijuana smokers everywhere (Indictment 2010-08-066-I). The filing is historic as it challenges New Jersey drug legislation and may change how the state's medical and criminal marijuana laws are enforced.

On April 1, 2010, Ed Forchion was arrested in Mount Holly, New Jersey, with a pound of cannabis in the trunk of his car. A Burlington County grand jury indicted Forchion in August of the past year for violation of the state's drug laws. In October 2010 he pleaded not guilty. He faces more than a decade in prison if convicted.

Forchion is a dual citizen of New Jersey and California. Forchion also operates a medical marijuana (dispensary) Temple in Hollywood, California, called the "Liberty Bell Temple II."

In December 2010, Superior Court Judge Charles Delehey permitted Forchion to challenge the constitutionality of the state's marijuana laws, which makes marijuana possession illegal (and a Schedule I drug) because it purportedly has no medicinal value. At the same time, New Jersey is implementing a medical marijuana program for the treatment of needy and ill citizens since New Jersey became the 15th state to legalize the use of medical marijuana in January 2010.

The legal brief raises eight grounds explaining why the indictment must be dismissed. These include that Forchion, as a practicing Rastafarian, should be granted a religious exemption under the First Amendment (and Equal Protection Clause) to possess marijuana since marijuana – known as ganja in the religion – functions as a sacrament and is an integral part of the Rastafarian religious ceremony.

Other issues raised in the brief are: that marijuana should no longer be classified as a Schedule I drug (with the hardest drugs such as heroin, LSD, etc.), since even New Jersey now recognizes its medicinal value; that Forchion should be able to possess the marijuana on the grounds of "medical necessity" since he is a medical marijuana patient (approved in California, one of his two residences); and that the New Jersey marijuana laws do not provide adequate notice that he could not possess his required medicine (and religious sacrament).

Saykanic says, "It's not only un-American that Rastafarians are discriminated against for their sacred religious views, but it's outrageous that the alleged 'illegal' drug that is their sacrament has now been acknowledged by the state to have great medicinal value, yet they continue to be persecuted."

Remember, I was diagnosed in 2001 with a form of bone cancer, but I kept it to myself. I openly talked of legalization, openly admitted I had a medical marijuana card and supported medical marijuana, but I kept my personal battle with bone cancer to myself. But fighting this NJ legal case made me publicly reveal my condition in October of 2011. I did it with these videos:

- http://tinyurl.com/videotumor1
- http://tinyurl.com/videotumor2

"I was scheduled to have a tumor removed on October 18, 2011. My recovery time would have been about 3-4 months. Because the judge had "denied" my pre-trial constitutional challenge http://tinyurl.com/challengeDenial at that time and I actually feared that I may be railroaded into prison, I went public. I didn't want to have another surgery under prison conditions either.

My surgery was supposed to happen in Oct 2011 but a few days before the surgery it was determined by the business office at Kaiser Hospital that they weren't going to offer it as a charity case. I then went to U.S.C. hospital and it was rescheduled for January 18th, 2012. Lucky for me on January 17th while getting ready for surgery I was offered a experimental treatment and I accepted. I didn't want the surgery, I didn't like the prospect of it coming back again and the possibility that it could come back in a dangerous place. So I was happy not to have the surgery and accepted enrollment in the experimental treatment drug Denosumab.

The goal and purpose of the New Jersey Compassionate Medical Marijuana Act of 2010 was to protect medical marijuana users from prosecution. Yet Judge Delehey ruled I couldn't utilize it as a defense or bring it up before my jury. He denied my Challenge Brief and denied me the right to present expert witnesses to perfect my medical necessity defense. Prosecutor Luciano didn't believe it. He made snide comments and was a limp dick, and tight ass about it."

This is when Burlington County Prosecutor Luciano sicced the DEA on Forchion. He found out later when he got a copy of the federal search warrant probable cause. (http://tinyurl.com/LBTfederalraid)

December 13, 2011, the U.S. Drug Enforcement Agency raids the Liberty Bell Temple II - http://tinyurl.com/LBTfederalraid2

The DEA cleared the place out, seized marijuana, drained his bank accounts, and boarded up his south L.A. grow operation. Weedman says it all went down December 13 at 11 A.M., when he was pulled over by the LAPD and the DEA was there to help.

He says he was taken to his Liberty Bell Temple II pot shop in Hollywood in cuffs as agents raided the place and seized everything in sight.

"It was a total smashing. They smashed all my cameras, they took all my computers. They smashed up my house. They took all my paperwork. They thought I still had an apartment in the Valley; they went there too and found out I didn't live there anymore. They went to my bank. They seized everything."

His south L.A. grow warehouse on Gage Ave. was hit too. He says an agent told him he would be in deep shit if they found 1,000 plants or more. As it was, they took 600, he said.

While Weedman says he was shown a search warrant, he says he's still not exactly clear on why he was raided and that he has been informed of zero charges or indictments. http://tinyurl.com/LBTfederalwarrant

His theory is that having his face in the news in New Jersey set off the feds at the behest of former federal prosecutor Chris Christie, now governor of the Garden State.

That DEA raid, "It fucked up my income, fucked up my life all over again. It was like 1998 all over again. I still said I'm not ever taking a deal again—if they're going to put me in prison, a jury will have to put me there." Not only did he lose his livelihood and possessions and have to surrender his apartment, even his dog had to stay with friends while Forchion fought this battle in court. He had planned to pay for his expert witnesses and legal help to fight his case. He left California in what he called a Roadamentary (http://tinyurl.com/videoroadamentary) on March 20, 2012, with no money—just an Internet-enabled phone—and Paypaled his way across the country in his new version of a WEEDMOBIL (http://tinyurl.com/videoArrival) to reach New Jersey in time for his trial date of April 1—two years to the day after he got arrested.

The trial started on May 1, 2012, and the entire region watched the public trial. Every newspaper, radio station, and TV station covered it.

The more serious charge of possession with intent to distribute resulted in a hung jury on May 9 and would subsequently be thrown out. But Forchion did get found guilty of simple possession. "I talked to a couple jurors and knew I had standing to appeal the issues. The prosecutor decided to put me on trial again." (Image credit Calkins media)

This was a huge victory—potheads across the nation saw this.

TRIAL 1 COVERAGE

- **(April 2012) PRE-TRIAL NEWS COVERAGE- If you were on my JURY what would you say? (SEE VIDEO)** http://tinyurl.com/nlmejep

- **"The Weedman heads to court "**
  http://tinyurl.com/headstocourt

- **"ALL EYES ON WEEDMAN"**
  http://tinyurl.com/NJWalleyes

- **"Jury selection to continue in NJWeedman trial"**
  http://tinyurl.com/NJWjuryselection

- **"Prosecutor: NJWeedman is a "charlatan ... a wolf in hemp clothing"**
  http://tinyurl.com/NJWcharlatan

- **"Trentonian TV: NJWeedman goes to trial"**
  http://tinyurl.com/NJWstartstrial

- **"No verdict in NJWeedman trial; jury to return Wednesday"**
  http://tinyurl.com/NJWjurytoreturn

- **"NJWeedman found guilty of possession; hung jury on distribution charge "**
  http://tinyurl.com/NJWhungjury

- **"Judge takes Forchion to task for trying to 'scuttle the judicial process' "**
  http://tinyurl.com/NJWscuttle

- **"THE VERDICT "**
  http://tinyurl.com/NJWverdict

- **"NJ Weedman vows to fight on"**
  http://tinyurl.com/NJWtofighton

- **"Jury hung in NJWeedman case"**
  http://tinyurl.com/NJWhungjury2

- **"NJWeedman asks court to set aside guilty verdict**
  http://tinyurl.com/NJWsetaside

- **"NJWeedman retrial to be moved to September"**
  http://tinyurl.com/NJWretrialset

In May of 2012 Forchion was found guilty of simple possession, which he viewed as kind of a positive because normally one doesn't go to jail for that in NJ, but it still allowed him standing to file a challenge to the entire law. "I'm set up right now to change the law in the state of New Jersey, without having to sit in a jail."

"For those several months (May to October) between trials I talked shit to newspapers, and the judge said I was trying to undermine the judicial process. I was regularly publicly explaining jury nullification on the biggest statewide talk radio—101.5 FM."

http://tinyurl.com/USCOLLECTIVE

"I also opened a new medical marijuana dispensary in Los Angeles. I called it the United States Collective (USC), and it was located directly across the street from USC General Hospital. I teased Luciano that I was going to name my new collective Luciano's Place."

"I had spotted a vacated building while getting cancer treatments at USC. I had obtained just a few dollars between trials – I tried to rebuild, to reopen to recapture my life………"

- **"NJWeedman to be retried on drug distribution in October"**
http://tinyurl.com/NJWretrialOct

By October 2012, Forchion was all over TV—as far up the chain as CNN: As far as the PR war was going, NJWeedman wins! No activist in the country commands a media presence like he does. The state of New Jersey may have prevented him from legally being NJWeedman.com, but the public knows him and accepts him as NJWEEDMAN.

TRIAL 2 COVERAGE

- "Do You Think NJ Weedman Ed Forchion Should be Found Not Guilty? [POLL]"
  http://tinyurl.com/NJWtrialPoll

- "'NJ Weedman' looks to plant a seed on his jury"
  http://tinyurl.com/NJWseedjury

- "Weedman seeking 'pothead' for his jury"
  http://tinyurl.com/NJWseekingpotheads

- "Weedman: 'I am conviction proof' as jury is picked"
  http://tinyurl.com/NJWconvictionproof

- "'Weedman' trial begins Tuesday, with or without him"
  http://tinyurl.com/NJWtrial2begins

- "Weedman Being Re-tried On Drug Charges After Hung Jury"
  http://tinyurl.com/NJWburlcobuzz

- "NJWeedman retrial begins"
  http://tinyurl.com/NJWtrial2begins2

- "Expert testifies on behalf of Weedman"
  http://tinyurl.com/NJWexpertwitness

- "Montco man arrested handing out fliers at NJWeedman trial"
  http://tinyurl.com/NJWmontcomanarrested

- "NJWeedman case to go to jury Thursday"
  http://tinyurl.com/NJWgoingtojury

- "NJWeedman found not guilty in pot distribution case"
  http://tinyurl.com/NJWfoundnotguilty

- "NJ Weedman Ed Forchion Acquitted – Almost a Marijuana Martyr [POLL]"
  http://tinyurl.com/NJWmartyr

- - "'I'm not a weirdo ... I'm a hero'"
  http://tinyurl.com/NJWImahero

- "'NJWeedman' acquitted, still faces prison time for possession"
  http://tinyurl.com/NJWacquitted

- "'Weedman' found not guilty of distributing pot"
  http://tinyurl.com/NJWnotGuilty

- "Jury upends marijuana law, NJWEEDMAN walks free"
  http://tinyurl.com/NJWwalksfree

On Oct 18th, 2012 the jury said "Not Guilty" and we went to celebrate at the local bar. While I was there I got a call from DEA Agent K. a female agent who was present during the Dec 13th, 2011 RAID. She congratulated me for the not guilty verdict but what she was really doing was telling me Uncle Sam was still there watching me. At the same time in Los Angeles a couple DEA agents showed up at U.S.C. and confronted my employees and stood outside taking pictures of my patients/customers. A few days later they dropped off a cease and desist order giving me two weeks to close and told my employees if they continue to show up for work they will be included in the Federal investigation of me.

The United States Collective was closed on November 04, 2012
http://tinyurl.com/USCOLLECTIVEclosed

SENTENCING

JAN 2013: Although Forchion was due to receive a stay of sentence upon completion of the trial until all constitutional arguments could be heard on appeal, the judge reneged: Forchion was offered probation instead, which he found intolerable for several reasons. Besides the obvious not being able to partake of an herb that was sacred to him (and, as we'll discuss shortly, that may have been keeping him alive and

well), probation meant he couldn't vote, and if he can't vote, he can't run for office, which he vowed to do every year to "give the finger to the system" until cannabis is legal. And though he was the only convict in New Jersey who didn't have to give up his DNA in 2003, now that the judge reneged on the deal, Forchion was ordered to surrender his DNA that day and sign up for probation, which he did not do. "I wasn't supposed to get probation."

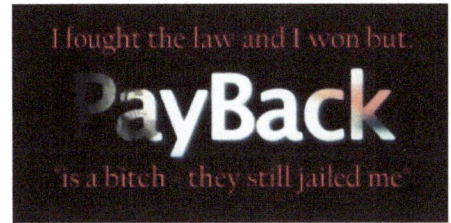

"During my pre-trial deliberations I had won that concession from Judge Delehey. Prosecutor Luciano and I had agreed that no matter what happened, I would get a stay of sentence. He got me not to do something in return! I was threatening to go to appellate court about certain constitutional issues. But instead the judge and prosecutor, for the sake of expediency, agreed that at the end of this case no matter what—if I were found *not guilty* I'd walk free, if not then the judge would agree to a stay of sentence until we went through all the constitutional arguments before the Appeals Court. I would not file an interlocutory appeal if he promised to issue a stay of sentence. So no matter what happens at the end I am not going to get sentenced. On sentencing day he reneged on the deal, and I was so mad I refused to sign the probation papers. A warrant was issued for his arrest. A week later he was arrested at the airport while waiting to fly back to California for his monthly cancer treatment (though he says he intended to return in 4 days and continue fighting his case). He spent February and March in jail in New Jersey. "They demanded that I plead guilty to violating probation, but I never was on probation in the first place. I never signed, they never got my paperwork. Probation didn't have shit on me. The judge was mad at me—yet he reneged, not I, and he treated me like I was "**Just Another Nigger.**"

- **Sentencing: "Two years' probation for marijuana activist 'NJ Weedman'"** - http://tinyurl.com/NJWprobation

"You see, they didn't expect me to win. They thought my argument that the law was wrong would fail and that I would go to jail. I won, there was egg all over their faces. I went to trial saying I'm a pothead, I'm conviction-proof, fuck the law, I only need one... They thought that was crazy in 2000 and in 2012. Well, I won, but I did get found guilty on a simple possession charge. You don't go to jail for that, you get probation. I didn't even want it. People talked shit to me: 'You had probation and didn't sign the papers? You chose to go jail?'"

Back up bitches who think that: I run for office every year. When you're on probation, you lose the right to vote. If you can't vote you can't run for office, and I run every year as a freedom of expression First Amendment thing. It's my way of giving the finger to the system. Him putting me on probation, that's the first thing I thought was 'fuck that.' The second thing was that I had fought the state successfully 10 years ago to keep the state from getting my DNA. Not only was I now supposed to give up my DNA—I had a horrible time with probation (ISP) before, it is a setup for failure to me, for the future. The judge reneged on the deal, so I fuckin' refused to sign the papers. The judge went ballistic because I refused to sign the papers, and he jailed me. On my way to get my cancer treatment! So I was pissed."

Now he faced 270 days in jail for a simple possession charge: "No one goes to jail in New Jersey for simple possession. If you violate parole or probation, you don't go to jail for a simple possession case! The judge reneged on the deal and put me in jail."

"My trial was unfair and the judge in other pre-trial rulings had made errors that we all knew would be overturned on appeal. Ultimately we all knew on constitutional arguments, denial of expert testimony, violations of my Sixth Amendment compulsory right to present witnesses…were all appealable. They were overturnable errors and he knew he made them, but he didn't care because he got some blood out of me by jailing me. On appeal I was going to win. Because I have a track record of fighting this and that and marijuana and constitutionality, the judge said on the record there are constitutional issues so no matter which way he decides, he agreed not to take my liberty until these arguments could be presented to the appellate court [because there was no legal precedent in a medical marijuana case]. He reneged, I went to jail."

Forchion says being found guilty in this case gave him standing to file an appeal—to question the law. During the buildup to the case, several constitutional arguments were raised, some of which had never been tried in New Jersey. "The legal landscape of marijuana is changing across the country as new marijuana laws are enacted. When New Jersey enacted its medical marijuana law in 2010, it entirely changed the legal landscape. For instance, NJ's 2C criminal statutes describe marijuana as a Schedule 1 drug having no medicinal value. But the very first line of the medical marijuana Compassionate Use Act says the State of New Jersey now recognizes that marijuana has medicinal value. This is directly in contrast with the state's 2C laws that say it has no accepted value. But the legal landscape changed, the 2C laws are from the '80s, and federal scheduling is from the '70s. This appeal is all new ground."

"Between the first and second trials of 2012 [May and the October], that's when Judge Delehey and I started battling. He began yelling at me about jury nullification. Saying I was trying to undermine the judicial process which is bullshit. I was simply encouraging my jurors to engage in Jury Nullification. It's legal to do it but these authoritarian type people who control our Government and legal system resent citizen oversite. NJ Constitution's article 1, paragraph 6 specifically states that: "*In **all prosecutions** or indictments the jury may be told the truth as evidence,…and the jury may judge the law as well as the facts in a case.*" This has been the most important aspect of Forchion's defense and the focus of the message he's committed to spreading.

The judge threatened Forchion with contempt. "I said something smartass like, 'Maybe you should charge me with having no respect that would be more accurate,' something like that.

"When newspapers were following me, I'd said I just needed 1 pothead, that I was conviction-proof. I was rubbing everyone's nose in it. I just got 7-5 in one trial, I was confident I could get 1 again. I got 12. It pissed them all off. I know in the beginning they totally didn't think I could pull it off. I always get underestimated by those types: suit-and-tie clean-cut white guys. It helps me actually when these types underestimate me because by the time they realize I'm dangerously intelligent and a worthy but eccentric adversary, it's too late for them." http://tinyurl.com/NJWplantingseeds

In May of 2012 Forchion was found guilty of simple possession, which he viewed as kind of a positive because normally one doesn't go to jail for that in NJ, but it still allowed him standing to file a challenge to the entire law. "I'm set up right now to change the law in the State of New Jersey, without sitting in a jail." Forchion accuses the judge of perpetrating "some fuckery": "The 270-day sentence was total bullshit. It was 20 days in, 10 days out, so I could continue to receive my monthly Denosumab treatment for my bone cancer. All told, I served between 130 and 140-something days. Every time I got out for 10 days, I was on a different show, publicly smoking weed and talking to press to criticize the state, talk crap about Governor Christie. Every 20 days the Weedman show began. The judge was embarrassed."

In August, between the two 2012 trials, the state elected to retry Forchion on possession with intent to distribute. The outcome of the trial in October: Forchion was found not guilty. "Between October and January is when again I was talking crap to all these papers with regard to jury nullification. So then I come to sentencing January 13; I was expecting a stay of sentence, as set forth during pre-trial arguments. The judge had agreed. So now it's January 17, 2013, and at the sentencing the judge reneged on the pre-trial agreement. I was upset. I refused to sign the probation papers—I walked out of court. The agreement was to keep me from going to appellate court on an interlocutory appeal, which would have slowed the case down and generated a bunch of publicity. We both had a bit to lose. I didn't want to keep dragging this case out. But I thought it was a valid argument I had, and everybody agreed. So I proceeded. He said basically that at the end of trial I was not going to jail, a stay of sentence would be issued. Then I win the big part of the case: first a hung jury on the charge of possession with intent to distribute, then not guilty. At issue was the new prospect of probation in lieu of a stay of sentence. But it is a loss of liberty—I had to give up DNA, I lost the right to vote and run for office, and I couldn't smoke. That's why I didn't run last year. So I don't sign it and I leave courthouse. And 11 days later I leave for the airport, that's when they get me. I didn't know I had a warrant. I intended to file a motion for consideration. I just knew I was not signing this, not giving up my DNA. I required the transcripts so I could prove my arguments. I needed to prove that I had an agreement. But then he arrested me and had me locked up, it was horrible."

Flashback to late 2009: Forchion feels a twinge of familiar pain again. This time he has an inkling of what it might be. There were no veins, just pain. Luckily it came back in roughly the same spot (slightly lower), rather than migrating to a more problematic part of the body like the lung or head. MRIs done in California confirmed the presence of another mass, but it was slow growing. After applying for charity care at Bob Hope Hospital and hearing nothing he applied for the same at Kaiser Permanente. All pre-operative procedures such as X-rays and blood work were granted, but at the last moment Oct 2011 before the actual surgery was to commence, someone in the business office realized how costly the procedure is and decided to deny it. "It turned out to be a blessing," says Forchion. Doctors from Kaiser communicated effectively with doctors at USC - University of Southern California. There one of the oncologists recommended he come to the Santa Monica Oncology Center and partake of an experimental drug treatment called Denosumab, which was being used as a treatment for osteoporosis but demonstrated pertinence for conditions of bone cancer. The Santa Monica Oncology center was testing a concentrated version of Denosumab on tumor patients. "I have a condition that, when they put me in the records at USC, docs come flyin' out of room like, 'Hey, we got one.' They were excited—I'm a toy to them, a novelty, because I have a unique condition and they don't see many like me. I have a condition that's both rare and not aggressive, so they can study me." Over time the monthly shot (which costs about $3,500, but which Forchion receives for free in exchange for being a "guinea pig") appeared to be working, and the prospect of not having to have the mass cut out (or receive an artificial knee) was a relief.

Denied medical treatment until I pleaded guilty

And so, Forchion was held for the month of February 2013. He missed his February 4 Denosumab shot

and then his March 5 shot. "The public defender and the Judge agreed to take me out of jail and bring me in front of the judge if I agreed to plead guilty to a probation violation. So I see him, he didn't want to hear shit I had to say except whether I was going to "plead guilty". If I had said anything else I wouldn't have been released to get my treatment. I was forced by the denial of my cancer treatment to plead guilty to a probation violation when I never was on probation. The judge lets me out, says he's going to reevaluate the situation.

Between the two hearings (March 2013 and Sept 2013) I talked to a lot of press about the situation that's when I did a Reason TV interview while in Los Angeles. http://tinyurl.com/videoReasonTV

I started screaming bloody murder about this denial of medical attention and judicial Renegging but nobody wanted to hear me. And I have court on September 10. I've already done 40-something days in January, February, and March. I was let out March 15 with notice to appear back in court on September 10. When I come back to court then, the judge has an attitude and everything. And that's when he sentences me to do 20 days in and 10 days out of jail each month. All the way until January 26. September, October, November, December, January: 5 months of 20 days in, 10 days out; 100 days, already served

45 [February and March]. The judge schedules the hearing for January 28, I did 143 days of the 270 sentence waives the rest. His stupid sentence was making national news, even FOXNEWS — Fox and Friends portrayed it as idiotic. It was making international news, this BS sentence. I think waiving the rest of the sentence came from higher up. I made the system look stupid. National newspapers, the AP—it was everywhere. They told me I didn't have to come back, I'm done. While I was in the Burlington County jail I was so mad at the treatment of Judge Delehey and his reneging on the pre-trail agreement

to "stay sentence pending appeal" — I filed a petition to change my name to Just Another Nigger — to reflect how I thought I was treated and to bring some attention to the issue of racism in the courts.

Good news March 14, 2014 my Appeal Brief got filed. It's going to take about a year, but I think I'm going win and have my simple my conviction for simple possession overturned.- http://tinyurl.com/NJWappeal

I allege that I had an unfair trial, some of my valid constitutional arguments were just rejected by the judge. An appeal is for the review of the laws accompanying a conviction. I challenged the constitutionality of the law, which I could only challenge from the standpoint of a conviction. So my case at this moment in history in New Jersey is the most important marijuana case ever. I have a chance of overturning the laws. I'm trying to get the state's criminal laws ruled unconstitutional. I'm trying to get the appellate court with my appeal to rule in favor of allowing out-of-state medical marijuana patients. My appeal could undo the current law."

"Back last year in March 2013, hearings made me miss cancer treatments. The judge said he'll let me out of jail if I agree to plead guilty of violating probation. I never even reported. The probation department never filed a complaint. The Administrative judge of the state Judge Grant interfered. The judge Delehey did it, and put me in jail when I refused to sign the papers. The judge agreed if I plead guilty to probation, he would let me out to go to my treatments. Here I am, a guy who never pleads guilty, who fights everything. They have all the power: Plead guilty and we'll let you out to get your cancer treatment, or maintain principles and get sicker. My guilty plea to the violation of probation was coerced, and a violation of my human rights. I have transcripts to back it up." (Read the Transcripts here: http://tinyurl.com/NJWpayback)

"I am considered a legal medical marijuana patient in California, I had a card at the time of my arrest. I came home Easter weekend 2010 to visit my kids for a couple weeks, I brought a pound of weed with me. I was going to be leaving again I planned to leave my stash for future visits."

Forchion Favors the Bold

Cut to 4 years and 19 days after his April 1, 2010 arrest, Trenton, NJ:

http://tinyurl.com/video420trenton2014

Forchion spearheads a marijuana legalization rally, bringing his battle—and about 200 soldiers—to the steps of the State House on Easter Sunday, which in 2014 happened to fall on 4/20. He made national headlines and his image went world-wide. He carried a cross on his back, with a marijuana leaf symbolizing both his persecution and the Crucifixion of the herb. You might say things came full circle, but of course Forchion is not done fighting. Who knows what the future holds. "I was working on getting my life back together. Driving a truck again, driving coast to coast, getting a divorce, moving to California, living life, all's well that ends well. Came home for a visit, caught the second charge, Act 2. Get arrested. Apprehended at the airport, forced to plead guilty for a probation violation. I didn't serve the whole 270 days. Now that that's over, now comes my turn. I'm on the offensive now with this appeal. And I think I'm gonna win, I'm gonna beat the state. I want to change laws. Like I said, it's a new legal landscape."

But before all of that, Forchion has to battle on another front: He has surgery scheduled for April 29, 2014, in California. But one of the dangers of getting the tumor cut out is, it can still come back, and if it doesn't come back in the same spot, it could come back in a dangerous spot. "Right now where it's in my leg, if it weren't growing, I don't think I would get it cut out. But it's growing now into my knee joint. I don't want my femur breaking one day. Breaking a femur on the stairs is how some people find out they have a giant cell tumor. Doctors recommend cutting it out. On Tuesday [April 29] they're going to try to get all of the tumor out, but if it can't be done to the doctors' satisfaction, they're going to switch the surgery to a knee replacement. It's a radical move, the cut occurs high up on the femur." Therefore when he gets knocked out on that operating table, he doesn't actually know if he's going to wake up with a removed mass or an artificial knee.

Despite the deck being stacked against him to such an extent, Forchion did get some lucky breaks. He was lucky enough to know of Dr. Steven Fenichel, the medical marijuana activist who came to see him in jail 2000 and alerted both Forchion and the prison staff that something is seriously wrong. The doctor also testified at both of Forchion's trials in 2012. He was also lucky enough to get in on the experimental Denosumab study. "Burlington County Prosecutor Mick Luciano called me a Charlatan, the prosecutor wants to treat me like a criminal. Here's this guy who has a medical issue, a doctor is here with supporting records. I couldn't get my Los Angeles doctors to come, it was too expensive and how could they justify leaving their Los Angeles patients to come to jersey to testify in a criminal marijuana case, so once again I got lucky that I happened to know Dr. Fenichel and he's an activist."

Forchion's Bone of Contention

Judge Delehey and Prosecutor Luciano's persecution prosecution violated the spirit and goals of the NJ Compassionate Use Act of 2010 which was to protect from arrest. "My health was unjustly harmed".

Marijuana slows the growth of tumors and can even make tumors shrink. "I have tumors!" This is backed up by science: Through the magic of biomarkers, THC has the remarkable ability to produce apoptosis (programmed cell death) in cancer cells while leaving healthy cells alone. Studies coming from other countries such as Israel (all the way back since the 1970s) bear this out.

Forchion discovered this for himself inadvertently. "I was a heavy [weed] smoker. I didn't know this mass was there for a few years, but when I stopped smoking weed in 2000 [due to incarceration], it grew incredibly fast. The doctors were shocked. This thing had to have been there for a long time, but while I felt something I didn't react to it until veins popped out and the pain became excruciating."

His recent anger stems from his belief that if he weren't serving the 270 days with the 20-days-in-10-days-out staggered sentence, his tumor would have been fairly stable. "I was getting the experimental bone hardener Denosumab, which was developed as a treatment for those with osteoporosis, but which over the course of the past decade has also come to be regarded as helpful for other bone conditions such as lesions, tumors, sarcomas, etc. In tests done on women with osteoporosis who also had bone growths, around 90% exhibited shrinkage of the mass or outright disappearance. The mass stopped growing, but the drug wasn't developed for that application. So in order for them to market and license it for that, they had to have a new study to get it licensed to treat people with these conditions. I happen to have one of those conditions. But I think I was helped at least as much by marijuana as by the Denosumab. When I had to stop smoking marijuana because of Judge Delehey's reneging and jailing, I still got Denosumab."

"I can't prove it, but I want to tell my anecdotal story. Last year (2013) in jail, I was supposed to get Denosumab every month. For two months I didn't get Denosumab and I didn't get any THC in me. I was in jail for February and March of 2013, then I got out. When I was out for four months, I had an MRI; there was no change, no growth, no movement—no nothing. An MRI in June showed no growth. To me the Denosumab is working, so I'm happy. I went on like that from 2010 to 2013. The surgery was up in the air, but since the mass was stable—no growth, no movement, no rush. I decided in a medical decision to use this drug along with the known properties of marijuana to retard my cancers growth. The doctors and everyone knew a certain percentage of these tumors that get cut out do grow back, and I'm already in that category. So I was happy not to have the surgery. It's all right, I'm not playin' ball anymore anyway, I'm 50 years old."

"BUT I got into a pissing contest with the judge though. He said I was playing my healthcare like a Stradivarius. So in September 2013, he (the judge) shits on me; does this whole 20 days in, 10 days out. But one thing was fucked up that no-one takes into consideration but me: Every time I'd got out for 10 days I'd get the Denosumab shot—and this was a crazy sentence that's never occurred anywhere else BTW—but during those 20 days in, *__I had no marijuana__*...the judge didn't care about my daily intake of marijuana." This to me was a denial of my medical marijuana treatment. Forchion asserts that each time he was trapped in jail and denied access to marijuana, his tumor grew like crazy. "As a result of not having my regular daily dose of marijuana for six months, I had 2 MRIs, in November 2013 and January 2014. When I went to see the doctor in February, I was informed of the results it [the tumor] was growing again. I immediately think that's because I got no marijuana. I can't prove it. Even the doctors say they don't just take one person, they'd have to take many people in a study—just like Christie likes..."

"I have all the paperwork to support everything. That's what pisses me off: The prosecutor calls me a Charlatan on the first day of trial and the judge says I'm playing my health care like a Stradivarius as he sentences me to 270 days in jail. Maybe if I were a bald-headed little white kid he'd take me, my condition and my treatment seriously. I look like a big angry black dude with dreads—neither one had sympathy for me."

On April 29th this Stradivarius playing Charlatan plays a concert – Surgery

http://tinyurl.com/429operation

Edward Forchion opens what he calls his "ganja-green eyes" after the surgery to remove the tumor from his knee on April 29, 2014. - http://tinyurl.com/NJWoperatingRM - He has made it, and the mass is out. "I'm actually happy I still have my own knee and the Doctor only took out the tumors". He was homeless in la so he recuperates at what he calls a "roach motel" tarted up to look like a recovery center for a couple weeks. He has managed to raise enough funds (no mean feat in his condition, since the DEA raid left him effectively penniless) to liberate his beloved Weedmobil from its los Angels storage-fee prison and soon is well enough to hit the road with two comrades from New Jersey to drive the van. (Not only does Forchion not currently have a license, the surgery took place on his right gas pedal leg.)

They cross the country in a couple weeks, documenting their progress and making stops along the way to visit friends and supporters. On Monday May 25th, Memorial Day, he makes it home to New Jersey. After a celebratory nap he went outside and—admittedly rashly—decided to move some of the bags from the Weedmobil. CRACK!

MEDICAL DIASTER

http://tinyurl.com/NJWbrokeleg

He was not supposed to put weight on it. A video on Facebook of Weedman down on the ground in agony, was followed by a video of NJWeedman in an ambulance on his way to the hospital. Several fractures! http://tinyurl.com/NJWambulance

He has medical healthcare in California, but not in New Jersey. Still, it was an emergency: Until he could get back to California, he was granted a cast at Cooper Hospital in Camden. And as soon as that cast was on, May 29th Forchion was out at a local Wawa campaigning, gathering signatures to get his name on the ballot to run for the 3rd District Congressional seat. Nothing would deter him even a broken leg from his goal of getting on the ballot.

The POLITICS of POT

He got more than twice the required 100 signatures to get on the ballot, factoring in some might be stricken for various technicalities. But when the other candidates caught a whiff of this, their parties levied an official cockblock against Forchion: They contested each signature in what would be an epic 15-hour stint in a courtroom. One by one they whittled down the names, removing individuals for the most trivial of reasons and sometimes—Forchion contests—errantly, until there were 97 names left. Three short of the required 100.

So he sued the Lieutenant Governor and the NJ Democratic State Committee. He continued to fight to appear on the ballot until a hefty (and arguably unnecessary) $3,500 transcript fee regretfully halted him—but he vows to mount a write-in campaign nonetheless. http://tinyurl.com/NJWtranscripts

"I'm not so high to think I can win, but I have enough name recognition to draw off votes. I'm better known than either candidate. I want to show that this issue is important to people, so politicians had better start considering it seriously."

In the meantime he is also taking his name change case to an appeals court. "I want to change my name to Just Another Nigger. If the courts insist on treating me like one, then I insist they address me as such."

Two casts, several weeks, and a lot more pain and inconvenience later, the breaks are healing, the cast is off. He still needs a cane to walk but hopes to regain his full range of motion and move on with his health. But his star continues to rise. He was over the moon when he was approached by *The Trentonian* to become a columnist for the publication, which is also read by the people who work in the state capital. He has an official platform from which to reach the people. He smiles as he recalls how he used to have to diligently seek out the press, and now they keep up with his movements and will reach out to him. He keeps moving onward and upward. This is Act 3, and it could just be the most dramatic one yet. Now that he's done defending himself in a string of legal persecutions, he is on the offensive—and he is enjoying the bullshit out of himself.

THIS STORY ISNT OVER

ITS CONTINUING

BUT THIS BOOK HAS TO END HERE

LAST THOUGHT

"JUST SAY NO TO CHRISTIE" VIDEO: http://tinyurl.com/Videonochristie

BONE CANCER PATIENT
PROSECUTED IN NEW JERSEY

By Alex Napoliello | NJ.com (Jan 3rd, 2014) Edward Forchion, known as "NJ Weedman," is using his 10-day grace period from jail to not only get treatment for his bone cancer but also to push his agenda against Gov. Chris Christie's possible run for president in 2016.

Forchion is serving a 270-day staggered jail sentence after being found guilty of marijuana possession following a 2010 arrest. He serves 20 20-day periods of incarceration separated by 10-day periods of release.

"Gov. Christie made a political point to be opposed to marijuana laws and cannabis laws and just taking a cue from the 'Just Say No' campaign, I figured I would put out the ads nationally to oppose Gov. Chris Christie's campaign for presidency," Forchion told My9NJ.   http://tinyurl.com/VideoMY9TV

Forchion is using his website (www.njweedman.com) and YouTube to promote his campaign against Christie. In a two-minute video, Forchion warns the marijuana-smoking community of the dangers if Christie is elected president in 2016.

"Beware cannabis-consumer community of America, there is a danger approaching – New Jersey Gov. Chris Christie will be running for president in 2016," Forchion said in the video with the iconic "Hollywood" sign in Los Angeles behind him. "He is a clear and eminent danger of rolling back the advances we have towards legalization, towards the medical marijuana reform movement of America."

In September, Christie signed a bill that allows sick children access to edible marijuana.

A medical marijuana facility – the third in New Jersey – opened its doors in Woodbridge on Dec. 4, 2013. The chief operating officer of the dispensary, Michael Weisser, promised to serve all 1,500 of New Jersey's registered patients, The Star-Ledger reported.

But Forchion doesn't believe the process is moving along fast enough.

"There's a backup. Even the new place that opened, it still takes a year for a patient to actually get his card and then get on the list," he told My9NJ. "There are patients who have had their card for over a year now who still don't have access to medical marijuana from the programs that are already open."

In 2010 Forchion was charged with possession and distribution of marijuana after a motor vehicle stop in Evesham. A jury acquitted him of the distribution charge but convicted him of possession. In early November he requested Gov. Christie to waive his jail term.

NO need to explain.......

www.ingramcontent.com/pod-product-compliance
Lightning Source LLC
Chambersburg PA
CBHW040750200526
45159CB00025B/1825